City under Siege

City
under
Siege

SONNETS AND OTHER VERSE

Mark Amorose

Angelico Press

For information, address:
Angelico Press, Ltd.
4709 Briar Knoll Dr. Kettering, OH 45429
www.angelicopress.com
info@angelicopress.com

Paperback: 978-1-62138-271-3
eBook: 978-1-62138-272-0

Cover design: Michael Schrauzer

for my mother and father

and

for all who defend and hand on the truth

ACKNOWLEDGEMENTS

I wish to thank David Middleton, Paul Lake, Catharine Savage Brosman, and Michael Carlin for commenting on earlier versions of some of the poems included in this volume. For their efforts to promote my work Joseph Pearce, Bill Haley, and Katherine Herrman have earned my gratitude. My wife, Maria, found time, amid the unending duties and demands of home-schooling and homemaking, to read and comment on each of the poems; for all she is and does I am ever grateful.

Some of the poems included herein were first published in the following periodicals.

Chronicles: "Floaters"; "*Carthago Delenda Est*"; and "The River"

Classical Outlook: "The Peltast"; "Pre-Socratic Philosophy"; "The Unbelieving Zacharias"; "To the Infant Martyrs"; and "Behold; We Were Seeking You"

Dappled Things: "The Mountains" and "Eusebio Francisco Kino, SJ: Apostle to the Pimas"

First Things: "Quebec"; "Cosmology"; "Spring"; "*Contra Mundum*"; and "By Their Fruits You Shall Know Them"

The Lyric: "Ant Lion"; "The Skeptic"; and "Confessional Poetry"

Modern Age: "Autograph Book"; "The Reason for the Moon"; "Vivarium"; "At Tyburn"; and "Fabre"

St. Austin Review: "Recusants"; "A Discourse on the Origins of Our Present Predicament"; "Eunuchs for the Kingdom of Mammon"; and "To Our Lady of Victory"

The Wanderer: "To a Paloverde Tree"; "St. Mark"; "Joan the Maid"; "Return to Cactus Rock"; "The Gates of Hell"; "His Brother's Wife"; "Easter Lilies"; "St. Francis de Sales"; "Mediatrix"; "Christmas Diptych"; "In Swaddling Clothes"; "Before Midnight Mass"; "And There Were Shepherds…"; and "Procession"

CONTENTS

I. Encounters

Quebec

Je me souviens.

The tourists traipse; the sights go by, a blur
of cramped and cobbled streets where faux cafés
and sellers of souvenirs administer
the sacraments of our despairing days.
Four-hundred-year-old churches punctuate
limp sentences of shops that line the ways.
The remnants of the Faith still fascinate,
and sunlight breaks through hedonism's haze.
We enter in, my bride and I: we find
the windows in a multi-colored blaze;
the altar soars before; pipes loom behind.
Outside the world winds down its final phase.
But pendant in the sanctuary's air,
the God we crucified calls us to prayer.

Cosmology

They told us that we lost our lofty place
when Galileo shattered Ptolemy's
concentric spheres, hurled Earth into the seas
of ever-growing, godless outer space.
They told us that the precious human race
originated in a cosmic sneeze,
dust specks upon a dust speck in the breeze.
They lied about our Father to our face.

If in a suburb of the Milky Way
man shelters in a modest cottage, he
must do so lest he love excessively
this paltry place, take breaking dawn for day,
or looking up adore the finite skies
and lose a universe that never dies.

Floaters

I listened—vision blurred, pupils dilated—
to the long list of all that was not wrong:
the macula had not degenerated;
the nerve was not inflamed; the lens was strong.
And yet the oculist did not deny
the swarms of spots I could not see beyond,
like paramecia that swim the eye,
ophthalmic protozoans in a pond.

Even the minute things in life can teach us.
See how these floaters in our field of vision,
by their very blunting of the eye's precision,
cut windows where the light of truth can reach us:
They tutor us how hard it is to see
the world with self-forgetting clarity.

Carthago Delenda Est

The city is beautiful. Off wave-lapped shores,
her gleaming merchantmen at anchor ride.
The wealth of all the world is in her stores:
the pretty and the priceless are her pride.
Her women are—as she is—rich and fair,
adorned as only queens in other places,
with gold and purple in their plaited hair
and condescension in their painted faces.

But luxury is purchased at a price:
a tax is taken; every woman pays
a tithe of blood for opulence enjoyed
so that the furnaces of Baal may blaze;
for mammon's cult demands a sacrifice.
The Carthage in our hearts must be destroyed.

First Sight

to my daughter Eleanor

I am a witness to a world of wonder:
Forests of clustered babel-towers try
to touch the heavens; steel birds stripe the sky;
dry asphalt tributaries rush and thunder.

Encoded bits of life take root: preplanned,
tall branching buildings grow from clay and shale.
Gray airships, flying low, fling strafing hail.
Wet autobahns speed through their beds of sand.

And here you are. All other wonders wane.
You wiggle on a pixel-painted screen:
two five-toed kicking feet are clearly seen;
two hands that flutter by a face are plain.
Ten weeks ago Another saw you, child,
and—never tired of working wonders—smiled.

Spring

I love to see the leaves arrive,
the new green spangling the blue,
when branches, struggling alive,
remake my window's skyward view;
or, looking down, to see the soil
pierced by the grassy vanguard's blades
and know that germination's toil
will end in flowered accolades.
And when I hear the shackled stream,
shedding its icy iron chains,
begin to live its dormant dream
and sing its rivulet refrains,
a hope wells up that there will come
another spring of Christendom.

The Mountains

The flatlands are our home: the fecund plains
with skies untouched by angularity,
roads rulered on a checkerboard of grains,
and rivers sauntering towards the sea.
What is it, then, that urges us to go
where bear-tooth summits tear a salmon sky,
where soil is stone, and cataracts don't know
that water's meant to flow but not to fly?

The mountains are the earth despising earth:
in one great striving, all of nature seeks
to leap above itself: even the trees
renounce round crowns for heaven-pointed peaks.
And we perceive our more-than-mortal worth,
ascending Rockies, Alps, or Pyrenees.

To a Paloverde Tree

Yours is a green that's never out of season,
that under summer's scourges never grieves,
a green that doesn't need a vernal reason:
You change not with the fickleness of leaves.
The desert's brown, the sun's gold, bold blue sky—
no other color can intimidate
that hopeful hue you hurl at the eye,
the green your trunk and branches radiate.

May we be like you in this arid age,
this desert that our dark desires have made,
where thorns of greed and heat of passions pain,
where lightnings lash and dry winds vent their rage,
that we may wear a hope that cannot fade
until the tender Heavens send their rain.

San Andreas

A colossal compass needle pointing north,
a mile-wide trench runs up the old *Camino
Real*. San Juan Bautista's church looks forth
upon a sight less threatening than serene. Oh,
for now, the giant grapplers in the ground
are resting. Yet the flexing of their muscles
foretells a fatal end to flinty tussles,
and tremors telegraph the final round,
when cities named for saints, but long apostate,
will tremble, and then, powerless and prostrate,
false heirs of Francis, flung from their proud place,—
like rude Antaeus torn from the embrace
of mother earth by godlike Hercules—
will sink into the purifying seas.

Autograph Book

This book was someone's treasure trove, a file
of paper fame and ink eternity,
an archive of the names that, for a while,
loomed largest and were sought most eagerly.
How heady must have been the hunting down
of household words, the touching of the hem
of fame, the acquisition of renown,
the locking up forever of some gem.

But ink will fade and paper wear to tatters,
the relic, like the man, return to dust.
All archives are in vain. This be my goal:
Against the world's decay, its moth and rust,
preserve the only autograph that matters:
the maker's mark inscribed upon the soul.

The Reason for the Moon

Within the vast Sahara of the sky,
the endless star-sand waste of outer space,
there is a sole oasis. You and I
inhabit this uniquely privileged place.
Here—here alone—the dance of night and day
sedately swings without a lurch or lean.
Here—only—life's impossible array
of elements decided to convene.

God hung a stony gray globe in our sight
beneath the shining desert overhead,
to signal us that all out there is dead,
that we alone reside with life and light:
that stars and satellites are poor and bare
while our inheritance is rich and rare.

Angels' Wings

Surely it was an adversary's plot,
or some blaspheming poet's simile,
picturing what most *is* as what it's not,
painting the height of strength so feebly.
So say not that you heard a rush of wings,
felt feathers fan the air or brush a cheek;
as soon say you caught sight of puppet strings,
or heard the clacking of a grackle's beak.
For angels are not birds. Imagine fire
acetylening blue before your eyes,
a wind that cuts your skin like diamond wire,
or snowmelt cataracting from the skies;
and pluck the feathered image from your mind—
but know these truer tropes still leave you blind.

The River

> How miserably blind was I to take
> This human span for almost-endless life.
> —Bocage

All day we drifted down the gleaming green,
following where the river ran ahead
to coil and lunge through meadow and ravine,
seeking the end of its predestined bed,

but we were at our ease, except to fend
off rocks or sidestep rapids, our delight
untrammeled as a ramble without end
down a road that ran before us into night.

The trees bent low above us to confide
their comfort—cottonwood and sycamore;
they hovered all along the riverside
like servants stretching forth the gifts they bore.

We gave no thought to route or destination.
The desert, with its cares, was far away.
We made our pilgrimage a recreation—
the hunt but not the taking of the prey.

But as day's heedless gleam died in the gloaming,
we stumbled on our terminus at last
and, unprepared, left off our pleasant roaming.
A cataract embraced us in its blast.

Ant Lion

Today I found a funnel in the sand,
a miniature Charybdis set on land,
constructed, careful grain by careful grain,
by some tremendous engineering brain.

And then I grasped how great this wayside wonder:
the tiny architect was dwelling under
the silent surface, waiting for a blunder
to send him splashing up to seize his plunder.

Who taught this little brute to build and mend,
to set his sandy trap to serve an end?
Sand-spouting, mandibled automaton,
who planned the patient course your life is on?

II. Victories

Vivarium

A.D. 540

Philosophy's last hope lies in his grave;
the grand plan of Boethius is dead,
bludgeoned by a brutal king. To save
our patrimony follow those who fled:
for Benedict is hiding in his hills,
building a city to contempt of self,
where fervent souls surrender their own wills,
in a monastery on a mountain shelf.
Your university is gone; the seed
must sleep six hundred years until its season
arrives—bright springtime of the schools. We need
you now to take the treasuries of reason
and fly this dying light. Cassiodorus,
keep alive the West's past wisdom for us.

St. Mark

One of the scattered sheep—a nameless one—
ran naked, fear-sheared in his startled flight,
when the wool-shrouded wolf out of the night
fell on the Shepherd's neck, and all seemed done.

A would-be missionary (sister's-son
to Barnabas), admirer of the might
of adamantine Paul, paled at his plight
and quit the worthy work they had begun.

But then there fell the shadow of the Rock:
The frightened lamb and failed apostle came
to hear the tear-taught shepherd of the flock
who knew his cure because he shared his shame.
And he refashioned Mark from lion's stock,
a bishop-martyr with a mighty name.

Contra Mundum

The world unfurls its flag of toleration,
issues its edicts of equality,
and he who bears the sign of our salvation
is banished as a public enemy.

As Athanasius when the world awoke
to find itself ensconced in heresy,
so we whose world must wear a harsher yoke
are called to Athanasian constancy.

We, too, may need to navigate a Nile
to dwell in desert solitude awhile,
with foreign tongue and unfamiliar face
endure injustice, exile, and disgrace.

Hold fast the Faith. Set swords about the Creed.
And call on Athanasius in your need.

Joan the Maid

A.D. 1429

Her king shrinks crownless in his self-constraint
while Henry's roaring lions still devour
the land of holy Louis' lily flower
and strive to free a title of its taint.
But down Domrémy's road in desperate hour
rides from her parley with her patron saint
the soldier maiden bearing heaven's plaint
and, on her holy standard, heaven's power.

In city under siege and countryside
Jesus and Mary gain the victory,
not for the house of Valois nor the pride
and pomp of distant Bourbon's monarchy,
but that the might of men may be defied,
and great ones counseled to humility.

At Tyburn

St. Robert Southwell †21 February 1595

Here is the promise God gave me this morning
early when the sun rose from his grave
while Topcliffe went about the town suborning
new witnesses—lord, lady, nurse, and knave:
Just as this growing golden disk ascending
cannot be held back by the bonds of night,
so is the present age of darkness ending:
When you awake again, all will be bright.
For finally your years-long imitation
of Christ through agony of cell and rack—
the Herod-queen, the cruel interrogation—
comes to a close in crucifixion's black,
and heavenward your passion-proven ghost
ascends, a golden lifting of the Host.

Recusants

Snuff the candles; strip the altar bare.
Drag the table from against the wall.
Fetch the lute; let laughter shake the air.
Pour the beer. Make merry in the hall!
Chalice, rood, and missal: all are hidden;
chasuble and stole are locked away.
Tight-lipped, do exactly as you're bidden;
make no nervous move that might betray.
Priest-hunters are prowling in the dark,
fiendish in their firm determination.
Listen! You can hear the mastiff bark,
harbinger of harsh interrogation.
No longer are we masters of our homes,
but keepers of domestic catacombs.

Eusebio Francisco Kino, SJ: Apostle to the Pimas

Pimería Alta, 1687–1711

On the rim of Christendom—strange, stony land
where rivers carve inverted mountainsides
into the ground, and living crosses stand,
green gospels bound in thorns—a rider rides:
the centaur-priest, the numinous vaquero
who bred ten thousand head to feed his flock,
the West's first cowboy, Christ-sent caballero;
his hooves cut highways in the torrid rock.
Following in the footsteps of his Savior,
he travels tirelessly the mission road
from Tumacácori to San Xavier,
the *Via Crucis* in an equine mode:
from Casa Grande to Remedios
God's horseman rides the Stations of the Cross.

Fabre

> You rip up the animal and I study it alive; …
> you subject cell and protoplasm to chemical tests,
> I study instinct in its loftiest manifestations;
> you pry into death, I pry into life.
> —J. Henri Fabre, *The Life of the Fly*

On his *harmas* in the valley of the Rhône—
his laboratory light, fluorescent sky;
his microscope, his unassisted eye—
a patient plotter watches all alone.
In what swift ambuscade does he lie prone?
upon what secret doings does he spy?
into what minute mysteries does he pry,
this sentinel of worker, queen, and drone?

All others lose the forest for the trees—
how could they not who lay the forest low
only to squint at stumps and count their rings,
as if life's tale is told by lifeless things?
Blind analysts of death will never know
what he knows who looks into life and sees.

Return to Cactus Rock

Mexico City, 1926

I hear the droning anaconda drum
that makes hearts rage and frenzied senses burn;
the sound of sacrifice cries in that hum:
the demon gods of Tlacaellel return.
Blood-Drinker, Smoking Mirror, Lord of Terror—
they clamor for their tributary feast.
Our land is sunk in darkness, steeped in error,
and no Cortes is coming from the East.

My brothers, seize your rosaries and pray
to her who crushed the serpent in this city
four centuries ago, to her whose pity
silenced the devil's drumming men to slay.
For she can quench the firebrands of Marx
and smother Montezuma's seeded sparks.

The Gates of Hell

Napoleon has come; the sentries sound
the tocsin. Battlefields are strewn with dead.
The pope is doomed.—But what is this? Like lead
the Revolution's guns fall to the ground.
"Pius the Last" was only the beginning:
Six namesakes later, Stalin smirks and sneers
at Peter's might. Then Stalin disappears.
Now ask the latest tyrant who is winning.

On Kephas, Petros, *Peter—on this Rock—*
I build my Church, forever to remain.
I give this promise: pestilence and pain
will wrack her, but she will withstand each shock;
and when it seems past certain she will fail,
then most, the gates of hell shall not prevail.

III. Skirmishes

The Peltast

The peltast was a light-armed skirmisher
who, like an irritating little bur,
got caught inside your clothing in the field:
not for him, the hoplite's heavy shield.

In poetry the peltast's counterpart
eschews the serious poet's ponderous art:
he flings off verses from his little harp;
but though his weapon's light, its point is sharp.

A Discourse on the Origins
of Our Present Predicament

If as a child you learned your catechism,
you understand about the primal schism
when Adam fell from grace, with this effect:
from birth we have a darkened intellect,
a weakened will, and insubordinate passions—
we shun the Good, enthralled by passing fashions.
For mind, a rebel to its sovereign Lord,
is helpless when *its* subjects seize the sword.

And if you studied well your history,
you know the passions' second mutiny—
how after the Enlightenment revolted
against the Maker, mind in turn was jolted;
how, following *les savants philosophes*,
Rousseau imagined man a savage oaf.
Thus history repeats the primal schism:
reason's rebellion breeds Romanticism.

Declaration of Independence

We're told today to "think outside the box";
but what if it is Jefferson's or Locke's?
Liberty's shrine, the creed of sacred "rights,"
pursuit untrammeled of earthly delights:
Are we allowed to doubt, dare we debate
the goodness of the gods our guts create?

Eunuchs for the Kingdom of Mammon

"Where wealth accumulates, and men decay."

Goldsmith's sad paradox is with us yet;
in fact, the situation's sadder still:
dollars, by nature sterile, now beget;
the human race is eunuched by a pill.

His Brother's Wife

When Herod hears the news, he jumps for joy
and kisses Salome, his almost-daughter;
Herodias herself begins to dance.
The happy couple laughs about John's slaughter.

For wasn't John self-righteous, arrogant,
and bigoted to put them in their place?
But now, at last, the Church has come around
and Cardinal Kasper taken up their case.

For who was John to judge them and their love?
By no means are they excommunicated.
The Eucharist is theirs to take at will,
for John is dead, and dogma is outdated.

Elation puts to flight their disbelief.
The Baptist is forever in disgrace!
For now, at last, the Church has come around
and Cardinal Kasper taken up their case.

No more are they excluded from the fold.
A true good shepherd is our Cardinal Kasper.
Now man can rightly take his brother's wife:
pursue, seduce, cajole, cleave to, and clasp her!

Their union is legitimate, somehow—
in fact, perhaps, a conduit of Grace—
since now, at last, the Church has come around
and Cardinal Kasper taken up their case.

Annibale Bugnini

In Rome they should have known him by his name:
the enemy descending with his brutes.
But to our guardians' eternal shame,
the harried faithful know him by his fruits.

Comment from a Nonconformist Age

You've reached the height of nonconformity:
you look, you talk, you think, you *are*... like me!

Pre-Socratic Philosophy

In Miletus a fellow named Thales
got his name in the weeklies and dailies.
"All is Water," he claimed,
even what burned and flamed,
like the sun and that comet of Halley's.

But though Thales thought water sufficient,
his successors all deemed it deficient.
So, earth, fire, and air,
they posited where
poor Thales' thought proved insufficient.

Out of all this material confusion
Anaxagoras drew a conclusion:
He saw that behind
all this matter is Mind,
and thus ended the atheist delusion.

The Skeptic

What unexampled irony!
(The skeptic can't dispute it.)
He's certain there's no certainty:
to say it's to refute it!

On the New Atheism

The fool says in his heart, "There is no God."
Then says it in his book and makes a wad.
What wiser fools we have than in the day
when atheism's gospel didn't pay.

A Just-So Story

Today I found an earwig in my bathroom
where there were only silverfish before.
I've found those scaly vermin by the thousands:
I thought today I'd surely find some more.

Imagine my surprise when in that chamber,
windowless and virtually airtight,
I found the silverfishes had departed
or changed into an earwig overnight.

I used to doubt that evolution happened,
but now, at last, these eyes have seen a sight—
three tails transformed by Chance into twin pincers—
that proves that Darwin, after all, was right.

Confessional Poetry

Confessional poetry is poorly named;
for when, in penitence, are others blamed?
But let the confessional poet once begin,
he's sure to repent of someone else's sin.

For the Birds

Just north of Tucson, in the shadow of
Picacho Peak, there live the birds I love.
No dare-gale skylarks, these, no hummingbirds,
no feathered muses who elicit words
of gaping awe or gushing admiration—
and yet they are the wonder of creation!

When next you find yourself out on *I–10*,
just north of Tucson—it doesn't matter when:
in winter's chill or summer's heat—you'll see
the only bird that merits poetry.
Forget the cactus wren, our dear state's pride,
and leave the runner of the road aside.
The bird you seek is hiding, safe from harm,
within the fences of an ostrich farm.

IV. Anthems

Easter Lilies

Where once a thistle crown and barren reed
mocked at the might of Christ the King and Lord,
the earth that held His fecundating seed
now brandishes the Resurrection's sword.
And barren altars, where the candles died
in darkness on three endless-seeming nights
when *Tenebrae* entombed the Crucified,
are lumened by a thousand living lights.
As One has risen, many shall arise
during the hope-and-fear-filled final hour
when Christ, like lightning, streaks across the skies
and men must heed the angel trumpet's power.
In these three lily-signs God is adored:
the flower that is trumpet, candle, sword.

By Their Fruits You Shall Know Them

Hard words, Lord Christ! For what good fruit bear I?
For all your care and tending, what my yield?
You gave me to a garden well concealed
and watered me from fountains set on high;
you fertilized me with a wondrous Food
and sent a Wind to strengthen and make straight.
How patiently you prune and pollenate
with an expert arborist's solicitude.
And still my good works fall to earth unfinished,
my produce often stunted, bruised, or dented,
the rot upon my nature's root augmented
by blights I brought and beauties I diminished.
In that last counting up of our good fruit,
Lord, grant I not be reckoned destitute.

St. Francis de Sales

Were you to ask, with Hopkins, who most sways
my soul to peace, I'd not respond, as he
did, with the subtle don of Oxford's praise,
nor turn back yet another century
to celebrate the teacher of us all
or his seraphic friend, the follower
of that first Francis who, becoming small,
became great. Much as each of these may stir
the heart or light the mind to endless ages,
another Francis swayed me with the sweet
honey of Charity pressed from his pages.
I ask his prayers, that one day we may meet
where life is held with an eternal lease,
and all are one in everlasting peace.

Mediatrix

Only the full of grace can summon love,
can win good gifts of God for helpless man:
thus maiden's *fiat* loosed the longing Dove
and set in motion His supernal plan;
thus at the wedding when the vats ran dry,
"They have no wine" called forth the master's first
miracle; thus beneath a blackened sky
her heart was pierced and his thorn-bound heart burst.

O you, who gazing on the great *I AM*
behold flesh of your flesh knit up with Him
in hypostatic permanence, who give
us Maker, Son, and sacrificial lamb
(God's glory fragile-framed in face and limb!):
win us the wine of grace that we may live.

Christmas Diptych

I.

Gray skeletons of trees scratch at the sky
to pick apart the dingy cotton clouds.
I brave the down-and-denim-shrouded crowds;
I brave the slushy parking lots to buy.
This shopping season dulls the sharp mind's eye;
this old, ungodly ceremony cloys:
a hundred thousand made-in-China toys—
five hundred thousand would not satisfy.
But when the wrapping paper's thrown away,
and everyman is staring at his screen
to see just what his little masters mean,
I'll give my mind and heart a holiday
by thinking of a picture I once saw,
Angelico's Christ Child upon the straw.

II.

The stable walls are painted with his light;
two holy visages throw back the glow;
above the roof the angels in their flight
descend to catch the updraft from below.
Fresh from the messaged majesty and fear,
some shepherds, cautious in their confidence,
around the corner of the hovel peer
to take full-face the sunrise radiance.

Behind them trees grow green; before them grass
and flowers leap up from rejoicing soil,
where helplessness illumines ox and ass
and poverty shines forth like flame from foil.
Here Love is born beneath a cloudless sky,
a Christmas gift beyond our power to buy.

In Swaddling Clothes

> And she brought forth her firstborn son,
> and wrapped him up in swaddling clothes…
>   —Luke 2:7

Before his feet walked dry-shod on the waves;
before his hands gave sense to ear and eye;
before his voice called dead men from their graves;
before his wish caused bread to multiply:
the Lord of all was first a speechless child,
deprived of power by his swaddling bands.
How mighty were those tiny feet and hands
when on her helpless God his mother smiled?

Already when the kings came from the East
to greet a greater king upon his birth
and fell down at his feet upon the earth
with gifts for God and sacrifice and priest,
Mary had wrapped up—as with festive bows—
the world's first Christmas gift, in swaddling clothes.

Before Midnight Mass

Out of the black, a burst of aural light:
the newborn carols that we, singing, pray
deny it is the middle of the night,
and in the dark we hear the break of day.

Each song-starved tongue, each fasting ear, revives,
prepared by Advent abstinence to feast:
From voluntary limits on our lives,
the manna of the music is released.

And thus we hark, and herald angels sing
the first noël—*in dulci jubilo!*
We walk with Wenceslas the servant-king,
following where the saint has marked the snow.
And when the organ sounds the starting chord,
we are in David's city with the Lord.

And There Were Shepherds...

Luke 2:8–14

A living beam of light fell from the sky
as if some searchlight worker on the ground
had heaved his apparatus up on high
to scour the earth for aircraft that were downed.

And there the angel was. And there great fear
that strafed each soul and laid each conscience bare
until a siren sounded in each ear,
and of the angel's words they were aware:

Fear not—behold—great joy—this day is born—
And then bright fire flowered all around
as if incendiary bombs had torn
the earth, or napalm grown out of the ground.

But suddenly the fear of heaven's might
gave way to heaven's peace: the airborne choir
proclaimed God's armistice with man, and Light
shone down a single beam of star-cast fire.

The Unbelieving Zacharias

Translated from Crashaw's *Epigrammata Sacra*
Luke 1:18

The father of a speechless babe you'll be.
This seems to you a dubious decree.
Therefore, a speechless father will you be.

And since you ask too anxiously a sign
To prove the promise, now you must resign
Yourself to asking with a silent sign.

To the Infant Martyrs

Translated from Crashaw's *Epigrammata Sacra*
Matt. 2:16–18

Pour out your smiling souls into the sky:
Your tongues will learn to speak as spirits fly.

Seek not maternal milk from earthly clay:
Your sustenance will be the Milky Way.

Behold; We Were Seeking You.

Translated from Crashaw's *Epigrammata Sacra*
Luke 2:49

In sorrow have I sought and seek you still;
But all your zeal is for your Father's will.

So many pains, all kinds of deaths, I know:
I mourn, I weep, I bear a mother's woe.

A Rattlesnake Remembered

I.

In Death Valley on an August afternoon,
when solar fires burned on in fevered sand,
and shadows smoldered like a blackened brand,
I met a rattlesnake upon a dune:

A sidewinder, as motionless as dead,
a neat, tight coil of rope upon a deck,
a sleek and khaki cable to the neck
where jutted out the pitted arrowhead.

I'd seen a hundred rattlesnakes before:
great buzzing brutes, leaf-mottled with the sun,
barring a mountain path, commanding one
to turn around and walk their way no more.

The silent circle in the sand before me,
so slender and so still was not as those.
The faint black flicker forking from its nose
seemed to insist that no ill will it bore me.

A tensioned spring can seem a harmless thing,
mistaken for slack wire—until it's sprung.
And venomed fangs can send a little tongue
to test the air for prey, waiting to sting.

Recall the storied smiling crocodile:
Appearances deceive, and serpents most.
I did not stop to parley with my host,
but gave a wide berth to his desert isle.

II.

Viper that long ago was left behind
to hibernate in desert memory,
see what provoked your thought to strike my mind:
the rope-coiled cable of a Rosary.

To me it didn't seem a decoration
to dangle at a dashboard, nor a wheel
of words for muttered mindless recitation,
but like a quiet coil of tensile steel.

It lay concentric-circled on a dune
of pillow, chain-linked vertebrae of stone
exposed, and at its potent head a hewn
quartz crucifix in prism colors shone.

I picked it up. It rattled out its warning.
The sun sparked solar fires along its length,
unwinding in the glory of the morning
and fanged with heaven's anti-venomed strength.

To Our Lady of Victory

Who is she that cometh forth as the morning
rising, fair as the moon, bright as the sun,
terrible as an army set in battle array?
—Cant. 6:9

O Star of Morning, saving Star of Sea,
commandress of Christ's militants arrayed,
O queen of hosts, we place our hope in thee.

No daring deeds without thy rosary
could win Lepanto's maritime crusade,
O Star of Morning, saving Star of Sea.

To thee, as well, we owe the victory
in every holy battle where is prayed,
"O queen of hosts, we place our hope in thee."

The sword of Charles, the crown of St. Louis
before thy serpent-crushing feet are laid,
O Star of Morning, saving Star of Sea.

When fallen throne or principality
assails our souls in sin's rapacious raid,
O queen of hosts, we place our hope in thee.

As ever prayed our fathers, so pray we
who fight now in the valley of death's shade:
O Star of Morning, saving Star of Sea,
O queen of hosts, we place our hope in thee.

Procession

A narrow street, a third-floor window: I
look out to see a singing crowd go by.
All dark within, outside there seems a light
as afternoon goes fading into night.
A bright parade though some are dressed in black
suits and in sober dresses. At the back
come millhands, in their steel-toed boots and jeans,
rejoicing to be freed from their machines.
Before the troop two little girls send showers
of pink and white from baskets full of flowers
to pave the path down which a frail old priest
carries his golden burden, like the beast
that bore to Bethlehem the living Ark—
the monstrance is a Mary! All my dark
dispersed, I dash downstairs to tag along,
happy to be the least in that glad throng.

Notes

Quebec

Je me souviens ("I remember.") is the motto of the province of Quebec.

Spring

This poem's first line was suggested by the opening line of Roy Campbell's poem "Autumn," which first appeared in his *Adamastor* (1930): "I love to see, when leaves depart,"

Vivarium

Vivarium was the name of Cassiodorus's monastery in southern Italy.

St. Mark

In the first stanza, I follow those who have suggested that the young man mentioned at Mark 14:51–52 is Mark himself.

Joan the Maid

Jesus and Mary: *Jesu Maria* was the motto on Joan's standard.

Eusebio Francisco Kino, SJ: Apostle to the Pimas

Pimería Alta (Land of the Upper Pimas) was the name the Spaniards gave to the region evangelized by Fr. Kino (now southern Arizona and northern Sonora). *Rim of Christendom* is the title of Herbert Eugene Bolton's biography of Fr. Kino.

Return to Cactus Rock

Cactus Rock: the Aztecs' name for Mexico City.

Annibale Bugnini

Monsignor Annibale Bugnini, secretary of the *Consilium* established by Pope Paul VI to reform the liturgy of the Roman Rite following the Second Vatican Council, was the chief proponent of the liturgical innovations introduced in the *Novus Ordo Missae*.

On the New Atheism

The fool says in his heart, "There is no God." (Psalms 13:1; 52:1)

Mark Amorose's poems have appeared in *First Things*, *Modern Age*, *Chronicles*, and the *St. Austin Review*, as well as in literary magazines such as *Measure*, *The Lyric*, and *Dappled Things*. A previous collection of his poems, *In the Saguaro Forest*, was published in 2012. Mr. Amorose lives in Arizona with his wife and children.